CONTENTS

18: Here, There & Nowhere
(Qui, laggiù e da Nessuna Parte)
19: We are Not Sheep
(Non siamo Pecore)
20: My Tinder Man
(Uomo Tinder)
21: One Tribe
(Una Tribù)
22: Are We There Yet?
(Siamo Arrivati?)
23: Point of View
(Punto di Vista)
24: Stairway to Nowhere
(Scala verso il Nulla)
(Escalier vers Nulle Part)
25: Dead Music
(Musica Morta)
26: I Try to Not Let My Dick Control Me
(Cerco di non Lasciare che il Mio Cazzo mi Controlli)
27: This World is Burning Fast
(Questo Mondo sta Bruciando Velocemente)
28: Cockroaches
(Scarafaggi)
29: When You Kiss Evil's Face
(Quando Baci la Faccia del Male)
30: People Do Not Want to be Controlled
(Le Persone non Vogliono essere Controllate)
31: Screw You!
(Fottiti!)
32: The Crying Song
(La Canzone che Piange)
33: Let the Music be your Master
(Lascia che la Musica sia il tuo Maestro)

CONTENTS

34: Making LO♥E
(Fare l'Amore)
35: The Big Sleep
(Il Grande Sonno)
36: Youth is a Mask (but it don't last)
(La Giovinezza è una Maschera (ma non dura)
37: Bureaucracy is an Atrocity
(La Burocrazia è un'Atrocità)
38: Birthplace (Origins)
(Luogo di Nascita (Origini))
39: Don't Let the Grass Grow Under Your Feet
(Non Fare L'erba Cresca Sotto i tuoi Piedi)
40: Plutonic LO♥E
(Amore Platonico)
41: Commitment
(Impegno)
42: RESPECT
(RISPETTO)
43: Sympathy for the Devil
(Simpatia per il Diavolo)
44: Sometimes This World Makes Me Crazy
(A Volte Questo Mondo mi fa Impazzire)
45: Freak
(Capriccio)
46: Living in a World of Make-Believe
(Vivere una Terra di Finzione)
47: Too Emotional, Too Romantic
(Troppo Emotivo, Troppo Romantico)
48: Make LO♥E Not War!
(Fate l'Amore non Fate la Guerra!)
49: "Turn On, Tune In, Drop Out"
("Accendi, Sintonizzati, Esci")
50: Today's Lesson is...
(La Lezione di Oggi è...)

Acknowledgement of Land & of the Traditional Owners of this Land

I would like to acknowledge the Gadigal people of the Eora Nation, upon whose stolen land I stand on today.
I recognise that this land was never terra nullius — the land belonging to these peoples was never ceded, given up, bought or sold.
I would like to pay my respects to Aboriginal Elders past, present and emerging, and I extend this acknowledgement to all Aboriginal and Torres Strait Islander people.

Another Brick in the Wall (part 2)

We don't need no education
We don't need no thought control
No dark sarcasm in the classroom
Teacher, leave them kids alone
Hey, teacher, leave them kids alone

All in all it's just another brick in the wall
All in all you're just another brick in the wall

We don't need no education
We don't need no thought control
No dark sarcasm in the classroom
Teachers, leave them kids alone
Hey, teachers, leave those kids alone

All in all you're just another brick in the wall
All in all you're just another brick in the wall

Wrong, do it again
If you don't eat yer meat, you can't have any pudding
How can you have any pudding if you don't eat yer meat?
You! Yes, you behind the bikesheds, stand still laddy!

Written by Roger Waters
Performed by Pink Floyd

CONTENTS

1: Human Interactions
(Interazioni umane)
2: Bloody WOGS!
(Maledetti WOGS!)
3: I Have All the Time in the World
(Ho Tutto il Tempo del Mondo)
4: Be Patient
(Essere Pazientare)
5: I'm Good in Bed
(Io Sono Bene nel Letto)
6: It's Not About How Big Your Cock Is
(It's about how big your HE♥RT is)
(Non si tratta di quanto è Grande il tuo Cazzo (si tratta di quanto è grande il tuo CUORE))
7: Divine Intervention
(Intervento Divino)
8: We are in control, We are Incontrollable
(Abbiamo il controllo, Siamo incontrollabili)
9: It's Just Pleasure
(È Solo Piacere)
10: A Brotherhood of Man
(Una Confraternita di Uomini)
11: I'll Make Every Effort NOT to Abuse You
(Farò Ogni Sforzo per NON Abusare di te)
12: Life in a Cage
(La Vita in una Gabbia)
13: Toxic Positivity
(Positività Tossica)
14: Freedom
(La Libertà)
15: Leslie, The Black Sheep, The White Wolf
(Leslie, La Pecora Nera, Il Lupo Bianco)
16: Island of Lost Souls
(L'isola delle Anime Perdute)
17: You Have to Live with Your Actions
(Devi Convivere con le tue Azioni)

Human Interactions

(Interazioni umane)

They're are funny to watch...
...humans, I'm referring to.
The way we behave...
...individually.
...with a friend.
...with a partner.
...with a LO♥ER.
...with an enemy.
...with a group.
...with a family.
...with their God.

What are they *saying?*
What are they *seeing?*
What are they *hearing?*
What are they *thinking?*
What are they *feeling?*
What are they *imagining?*

Do they really *speak?*
Do they really *see?*
Do they really *hear?*
Do they really *think?*
Do they really *feel?*
Do they really *imagine...*
...what could be?
Do they really LO♥E?

"The Don"
05.02.2022

Bloody WOGS!

(Maledetti WOGS!)

We're too loud.
We talk with our hands.
We don't respect rules.
We don't respect the law.
We write our own.
In fact, we have our own giver of punishment...
...the Mafia.
We are those...
...*bloody WOGS!*

We create chaos.
We're anarchic.
We're anarchists.
We do what the fuck we want.
We don't give a shit.
We have our own code.
We are those...
...*bloody WOGS!*

You can either join us or...
...be against us.
We don't need you, anyway!
It is you who need us.
We are the ones that make you.
We are the excitement.
We are the energy.
We are the *POWER*.
We are the *creative force*.
Yep...
...those...
...*bloody WOGS!*

(WOGS is a derogatory term for Southern European immigrants used in Australia during the 1960s & 1970s)

"The Don"
06.02.2022

I Have All the Time in the World
(*Ho Tutto il Tempo del Mondo*)

Time *doesn't matter to me.*
Time *is an illusion.*
Time is fake.
Time doesn't *impinge on me.*
Time doesn't *affect me.*
Time doesn't *control me.*
Time *doesn't dictate me.*
Time doesn't *tell me what to do.*
Because...
...*I have all the time in the World.*

I am free *of Time.*
I am free from its *web.*
I am free from its *grasp.*
I am free from its *hold.*
I am free from its *power.*
Because...
...*I have all the time in the World.*

I have all the time in the World.

I have all the time in the World.

"The Don"
06.02.2022

Be Patient

(Essere Pazientare)

Be *calm*.
Be *peaceful*.
Be *restful*.
"All good things come to those that wait".
"All in good time!"
Just...
...be patient!

Be *tranquil*.
Be *positive*.
Be *easy*.
"Everything works out in the end!"
"Give it time!"
"Give it space!"
Just...
...be patient!

It's not *easy*.
It's not *quick*.
It's not *guaranteed*.
It's not *a certainty*.
It's not *a "done deal"*.
But it could be.
If you just...
...be patient!

That's all you have to do.
Be patient!

And everything will work!

But not necessarily the way you want it to!

"The Don"
07 02.2022

I'm Good in Bed

(Io Sono Bene nel Letto)

I'll *show you a good time.*
I'll *excite you.*
I'll *give you pleasure.*
I'll *take you HIGH.*
I'll *BLOW your mind.*
I'll *give you ecstasy.*
I'll *give you a wild time.*
I'll *make LO♥E to you.*
Because...
...*I'm good in bed.*

I'll *put your needs first.*
I'll *pleasure you first.*
I'll *focus on your desires.*
I'll *fulfill your desires.*
I'll *pleasure you without limits.*
I'll *connect with you & we'll become one.*
I'll *make LO♥E with you.*
Because...
...*I'm good in bed.*

I'll *make you feel.*
I'll *arouse passions inside you.*
I'll *satisfy your every desire.*
I'll *be sensual.*
I'll *get you aroused.*
I'll *make you "come".*
I'll *make LO♥E to you.*
Because...
...*I'm good in bed.*

"The Don"
07.02.2022

It's Not About How Big Your Cock Is

(It's about how big your HE♥RT is)
(Non si tratta di quanto è Grande il tuo Cazzo (si tratta di quanto è grande il tuo CUORE))

You're a man.
You've got machismo.
You've got all the moves.
You've said all the right things.
You should...
...you've said them often enough.
You know a way to a woman.
You know your power.
It's because you believe you have a big cock.
But you should realise...
...it's not about how big your cock is.
...it's about how big your HE♥RT is.

You have the looks.
You have the swagger.
You have the attitude.
You have the tatts...
...all over your body.
You have the shaved head.
You have the big cock...
...or so you think!
But you don't have the most important thing...
...a big HE♥RT!
Because...
...it's not about how big your cock is.
...it's about how big your HE♥RT is.

You think you're God's gift to women.
You're on Tinder.
In fact, you're a big hit.
You think you've got it all.
Especially your big cock!
But...
...it's not about how big your cock is.
...it's about how big your HE♥RT is.

Actually, do you even have a HE♥RT?

"The Don"
08.02.2022

Divine Intervention

(Intervento Divino)

Its Heaven sent.
It's an elixir of youth.
It has a special ingredient...
...the *"Green Fairy"*.
...*Absinthe*.
It's the drink for very special people.
It's Valentina's drink of choice.
When she wants to feel...
...heavenly.
Especially when she wants some...
...*"Divine Intervention"*.

Do you want *eternal life*?
Do you want *everlasting beauty*?
Do you want *immortality*?
Do you want to *remain young*?
Do you want to *live forever*?
Do you want to *go to Heaven*?
If you do...
...you will need to drink some...
...*"Divine Intervention"*.

"The Don"
08.02.2022

We are in control, We are Incontrollable
(Abbiamo il controllo, Siamo incontrollabili)

We are *fallible*, we are *infallible*.
We are *famous*, we are *infamous*.
We are *calm*, we are *becalmed*.
We are *fidels*, we are *infidels*.
We are *sane*, we are *insane*.
We are *rational*, we are *irrational*.
We are *logical*, we are *illogical*.
We are *relevant*, we are *irrelevant*.
We are *sympathetic*, we are *unsympathetic*.
We are *abled*, we are *enabled*.
We are *abled*, we are *disabled*.
We are *acceptable*, we are *unacceptable*.
We are *sympathetic*, we are *unsympathetic*.
We are *just*, we are *unjust*.
We are *legal*, we are *illegal*.
We are *couth*, we are *uncouth*.
We are *secure*, we are *insecure*.
We are *combobulated*, we are *discombobulated*.
We are *real*, we are *unreal*.
We are *unreal*, we are *surreal*.
We are *decisive*, we are *indecisive*.
We are *credible*, we are *incredible*.
We are in *control*, we are *incontrollable*.

But when opposites collide...
...it always ends up in violence.

"The Don"
09.02.2022

It's Just Pleasure

(È Solo Piacere)

It's *nothing more than that*.
It's *not that deep*.
It's *not that profound*.
It's *not going to last*.
It's *not LO♥E*.
It's just pleasure.

It is *temporary*.
It is *instantaneous*.
It *doesn't last*.
It is *transitional*.
It's *an instant of "self-gratification"*.
And then it's gone.
Because...
...it's just pleasure.

Don't become *addicted*.
Don't become *trapped*.
Don't be *enchanted*.
Don't be *caught up in its web*.
Don't *be caught up in its net*.
Because...
...it's just pleasure.

Don't get *confused*.
You will be *let down*.
You will be *disappointed*.
You will be *saddened*.
You will be *left empty*.
It's *not LO♥E*.
Because...
...it's just pleasure.

But enjoy it when you get the opportunity.

"The Don"
11.02.2022

A Brotherhood of Man

(Una Confraternita di Uomini)

That's what we are *seeking*.
That's what we are *searching for*.
That's what *we need*.
That's what we *have to build*.
A *"Brotherhood of Man"*.

Everyone, *holding hands*.
Everyone, *bound together*.
Everyone *connected*.
Everyone *full of LO♥E*.
Everyone part of a *"Brotherhood of Man"*.

It's not that hard to *imagine*.
It's not that hard to *do*.
It's not that hard to *build*.
It's not that hard to *have*...
...a *"Brotherhood of Man"*.

Yep, a *"Brotherhood of Man"*.

A *"Brotherhood of Man"*.

That's all we need.

A *"Brotherhood of Man"*.

"The Don"
11.02.2022

I'LL MAKE EVERY EFFORT NOT TO ABUSE YOU
(Farò Ogni Sforzo per NON Abusare di te)

I'll try not to *use you*.
I'll try not to *possess you*.
I'll try not to *control you*.
I'll try not to *reject you*.
I'll try not to *refuse you*.
I'll try not to *manipulate you*.
I'll try not to *belittle you*.
I'll try not to *put you down*.
I'll try not to *degrade you*.
I'll try not to *disrespect you*.
I'll try not to *dehumanise you*.
I'll try not to *treat you as an object*.
I'll try not to *objectify you*.
I'll try not to *monopolise you*.
I'll try not to *hurt you*.
I'll try not to *abuse you*.
I'll make EVERY effort not abuse you.

That's the best I can do.
This is ALL I can do!

I'll make EVERY effort not abuse you.

But I'll try REALLY hard!!

"The Don"
12.02.2022

Life in a Cage

(La Vita in una Gabbia)

We *are born into one*.
We *live our whole lives in one*.
We *die in one*.
That's life in a cage.

We can never escape.
Many have tried.
All have died.
They all failed.
But I still admire them for trying.
For trying to breakout of...
...living life in a cage.

There's no use *fighting it*.
There's no use *in denying it*.
There's no use in *running away from it*.
There's no use not accepting that...
...we all live life in a cage.

"The Don"
12.02.2022

Toxic Positivity

(Positività Tossica)

It's FAKE!
How friends do have on Instagram?
How many followers do you need?
What do you get from the robots?
FAKE Positivity.
You are allowed to be sad.
Because not everyone shines like a diamond all the time.

They don't wanna hear your complaints.
They don't want to know how you feel.
They don't give a fuck about your feelings.
Who are they anyway…?
…at the end of the day?

Be cool, wise and beautiful.
LO❤E yourself more than anybody else.
Get fit, travel, change your game.
You are more than what you think you are!

Miriam + "The Don"
12.02.2022

Freedom

(La Libertà)

What is freedom?

How should I act?
What should I do?
How should I behave?
How should I treat people?

Don't tell someone what to *think*.
Don't tell them what to *feel*.
Don't tell them what to *do*.
Don't tell them what to *imagine*.
Don't tell them what to *be*.
Don't *confine* people.
Don't *define* people.
Just let them express themselves...
...freely.
Without *restrictions*.
Without *limits*.
Without *boundaries*.
Without *controls*.
Is this even possible?

"*But what if they want to be VIOLENT?*"
I hear you ask in protest.

Oh, this is the oldest misunderstanding.
This is the justification that's always used.
To NOT allow people to be free.
Because...
...they will be violent!

But on the contrary...
...restricting someone's freedom is the violence!
By not allowing people to be themselves...
...this is violence.
We are all subjected to violence & oppression every day
Because...
...we are not allowed to express ourselves freely.
...independently.
...without fear.
...without reprisals.
...without being rejected.
... without being put down.

This is freedom.
To not tell someone what to *think*.
To not tell them what to *feel*.
To not tell them what to *do*.
To not tell them what to *imagine*.
To not tell them what to *be*.
To let them express themselves...
...freely.
Without *restrictions*.
Without *limits*.
Without *boundaries*.
Without *controls*.

It can be done...
...if we *believe in each other*.
If we *respect each other*.
If we *care for each other*.

Then...
...and only then will there be FREEDOM!

"The Don"
14.02.2022

Leslie, The Black Sheep, The White Wolf
(Leslie, La Pecora Nera, Il Lupo Bianco)

She's a *waif*.
She's an *innocent child*.
She's *beautiful*.
She's *cute as hell*.
She's *smart*.
She's *curious*.
She's *confused*.
She's a *free spirit*.
She's Leslie, The Black Sheep, The White Wolf.

She's *SuPeR COOL*.
She's *French*.
She's *exotic*.
She's *in LO♥E with life*.
She's *got a big HE♥RT*.
She's a *lost soul*.
She's a *wanderer*.
She's a *traveller*.
She's Leslie, The Black Sheep, The White Wolf.

She's *CRAAAAAAZZZZZZZZYYYY!*
She's *wild*.
She's *carefree*.
She's a *flowerchild*.
She's *born "out of time"*.
She's a *"child of the Universe"*.
She's a *"Cancer"*.
She's a *crab*.
She's a *"Moon-child"*.
She's Leslie, The Black Sheep, The White Wolf.

She knows a lot of people but she remembers no one.

"The Don"
17.02.2022

Island of Lost Souls
(L'isola delle Anime Perdute)

Planet Earth...
...alone.
In an ever expanding Universe.
An island.
Isolated.
Orbiting a star...
..."Sol".
In the *darkness*.
In the *vastness*.
In the *expanse*.
In the *cosmos*.
Is there anybody out there?
Or are we all alone?
Will we ever find out?
Are we just living on...
...*an island of lost souls?*

Never knowing why we are here.
Never having a clue of our purpose.
Never being a part of something bigger.
All alone.
In the vastness of space.
Is this all there is?
Are we doomed to be forever isolated?
Forever...
...*an island of lost souls?*

"The Don"
17.02.2022

You Have to Live with Your Actions
(Devi Convivere con le tue Azioni)

Be care what you *do*.
Be care what you *say*.
Be careful what you *think*.
Be careful what you *feel*.
Be careful what you *imagine*.
Be care what you *want*.
Be careful what you *desire*.
Be care what you *seek*.
Be careful what you *preach*.
Be careful who you *are*.
Be careful who you *want to be*.
Be careful what you *become*.
Be careful what you *aspire for*.
Be careful what you *dream*.
Be careful who you *fear*.
Be careful what you *fear*.
Be careful who you *hate*.
Be careful who you LO❤E.
Just be careful.
Because...
...*you have to live with your actions*.
...for the rest if your life!

BUMMER!!!

"The Don"
18.02.2022

Here, There & Nowhere

(Qui, laggiù e da Nessuna Parte)

Where are *you*?
Where have you *been*?
Where are you *going*?
You are *"Here"*.
You are *"There"*.
You are *"Nowhere"*!

Stop *struggling*.
Stop *fighting*.
Stop *panicking*.
Stop *freaking out*.
Stop *crying*.
Stop being *sad*.
Stop being *lonely*.
Stop being *only*.
Accept that...
...you are *"Here"*.
...you are *"There"*.
...you are *"Nowhere"*!

"The Don"
19.02.2022

We are Not Sheep

(Non siamo Pecore)

I am not a *sheep*.
You are not a *sheep*.
We are not sheep.

We do not need to be *led*.
We do not need to be *controlled*.
We don't need to be told what to *do*.
We don't need to be told what to *think*.
We don't need to be told what to *feel*.
We don't need to be told what to *imagine*.
We don't need to be told how to *live*.
We don't need to be told where to *live*.
We don't need to be told how to *behave*.
We don't need *leaders*.
We do not need *governments*.
We do not need *police*.
We do not need *armies*.
We do not need *weapons*.

I am not a *sheep*.
You are not a *sheep*.
We are not sheep.

So...
...do NOT treat me like one!

"The Don"
19.02.2022

My Tinder Man

(Uomo Tinder)

I went out with a *"Tinder Man*.
He seemed nice enough.
He said all the right things.
He said I was beautiful.
He said that I should be a *"Bond Girl"*.
That was a bit cliched.
But I let it slide.
We met at the *"Marley"*.
"The Marlborough", in Newtown...
...for those who are not of the *"Inner west"* of Sydney.
My *"Tinder Man"*.

He was a lot shorter than I had expected.
I had imagined someone taller.
He told me he was into music.
"This is good", I thought.
I like music.
He said he was an audio engineer.
I liked that.
That seemed really cool.
And that he recorded a lot of new *"indie"* groups.
I was impressed.
He showed me some of his work.
It seemed good enough...
...although a bit unoriginal & derivative.
But I was nice.
I lied...
...I said that I liked it.
He seemed pleased.
The night was going well...
...*my night with my "Tinder Man"*.

He said. *"Wanna come back to my place?"*.
I thought to myself...
...should I?
Why not I decided.
So, we went outside.
He had a sporty car...
...a BMW, I think.
I'm not that good with cars.
His place was very nice.
An old terrace house that had been tastefully renovated.
He showed me around.
He was very proud of his recording studio.
He showed me all the equipment.
And said that this is where he worked from.
We had a few more drinks.
With my "Tinder Man".

I didn't particularly like him...
...but I was feeling *"horny"*...
...I hadn't had sex for a while.
So, I decided, why not?
We kissed.
He tasted of mould.
But I had made up my mind.
And I wasn't going to let a mouldy tasting mouth deter me.
I don't do much kissing anyway.
So, we fucked.
It was ok.
Nothing to write home about.
My night with my "Tinder Man".

Will I see him again?
Probably not.
I'll see how I feel.

"The Don"
19.02.2022

One Tribe
(Una Tribù)

We are all one.
There are no *differences*.
There is no *separation*.
There is no *"us & them"*.
We are all in this together.
There is only *"one tribe"*...
...the *"Human Tribe"*.

One *family*.
One *society*.
One *race*...
...*the human race*.
One *humanity*.
One *world*.
One *planet*...
...*Earth*.
One *tribe*...
...the *"Human Tribe"*.

Unity.
Commonality.
Cohesiveness.
Solidarity.
Harmony.
Oneness.
"One tribe"...
...the *"Human Tribe"*.

Let's *hold hands*.
Let's *connect*.
Let's *hear*.
Let's *touch*
Let's *feel*.
Let's *LO*♥*E*...
...*one another*.
"One tribe"...
...the *"Human Tribe"*.

We are all "one tribe"!

"The Don"
21.02.2022

Are We There Yet?

(Siamo Arrivati?)

Where are we going?
What is our destination?
When are we gonna get there?
Will we be late?
Is there anybody else going?
When will we get there?
Is it very far?
How long will it take?
When will we get there?
How will we know when we have arrived?
Will anybody meet us?
Will I have someone to play with?
Will I like them?
Will they like me?
Do I look good in these clothes?
Should I get changed before we get there?
How do I look?
Will it be hot?
Where is that we're going?
How long will it take again, I've forgotten?
How will we know when we get there?
Is it well signposted?
Will there be food there?
And drinks?
Can you wake me up when we're there?
Are we there yet?

"No!"

"The Don"
22.02.2022

Point of View

(Punto di Vista)

Perception.
Subjectivity.
Perspective.
Different eyes.
Different angle.
Culture.
Cultural background.
Socio-economic.
Socio-economic environment.
Politics.
Political background.
Family.
Family background.
Gender.
Gender bias.
Biology.
Nature.
Nature verses nurture.
Orientation.
Curiosity.
Intellectual curiosity.
Interests.
Spiritual.
Religious.
Ways of seeing.
Different ways of seeing.
Different perspective.
Different *"Point of View"*.

It all about your "Point of View"!

"The Don"
23.02.2022

Stairway to Nowhere

(Scala verso il Nulla)
(Escalier vers Nulle Part)

Les courbes ondulées de l'acier
Je suis effrayée et attirée
Les traverser' les monter
Je ne sais ce qu'il m'attend
Mais je sais que c'est insensé
Penser y trouver la liberté
Un amour innespiré
Un souvenir oublié
Une joie qui cest effacée
Une amitié qui cest perdu dans le temps

Do you know where you are going?
Why do you keep climbing?
What are you searching for?
What is it that you're looking to find...?
...behind the door?
As you climb up the *"Stairway to Nowhere"*.

Faut il continuer a esperer
Ou tout simplement y aller
Mes esperences mes espoirs
Me font broire du noir
Je ne sais plus ce que je cherche
Je ne sais plus ce que jespère
A larrivée la porte sera t elle ouverte?

Maybe there is no *"Heaven"* above us...
...no *"Hell"* below us.
Maybe there is only sky.
So, what then?
Will you still keep climbing...?
...your *"Stairway to Nowhere"*?

Je veux etre un renard pas un clochard.
Manger du patté sur mon Canapé
Finir échoué comme mobidique avec la trique
Sans me soucier d'envoyer une rente a mémé

Pour mon cartier
Revenir au ronsard assis sur le trautoire
Manger des chips au city avec largent de madame Bray
Pas finir comme Alex a 25 ans SDF
Sans oublier Sadjo et Mama qu'il finiront surment avec une jélaba

Do you imagine paradise?
Do you philosophise about...
....*God?*
...*mortality?*
...*death?*
...*The Devil?*
As you climb your *"Stairway to Nowhere"*.

Laurie, Davide + "The Don"
24.02.2022

Dead Music

(Musica Morta)

It's the sound of *silence*.
It's the sound of *emptiness*.
It's the sound of the *"Nothingness"*.
What is that music that I don't hear...?
...it's the sound of *"Dead Music"*.

It's the sound of *suffering*.
It's the sound of the *"Non-Living"*.
It's the sound of the *"Abyss"*.
It's the sound of *servitude*.
It's the sound of the *"Brain-dead"*.
It's the sound of a *"Dead HE♥RT"*.

"The Don"
24.02.2022

I Try to Not Let My Dick Control Me
(Cerco di non Lasciare che il Mio Cazzo mi Controlli)

Keep it under control.
Don't let it take over.
It wants to *have its own way*.
It wants to *dominate me*.
It wants to *overpower me*.
But...
...*I try to not let my dick control me.*

It is very *powerful*.
It is very *strong*.
It is very *persuasive*.
It is very *controlling*.
It is very *dominating*.
If you let it be.
But...
...*I try to not let my dick control me.*

It waits until you are *weak*.
It waits until you are *susceptible*.
It lurks in the shadows...
...waiting for its opportunity.
It lays dormant...
...waiting for its chance to pounce.
With the speed of a cheetah.
It latches onto you.
It will not let go easily.
You will have to struggle.
You will have to fight it.
That is why I am always ever vigilant...
...*and I try to not let my dick control me.*

But it's not easy...
...and sometimes I lose.

"The Don"
25.02.2022

This World is Burning Fast

(Questo Mondo sta Bruciando Velocemente)

There's no place to *run to*.
There's no place to *hide*.
What'ya gonna do?
Do have an escape plan?
Because...
...this world is burning fast.

You can't *ignore it*.
You can't *close your eyes to it*.
You can't *cover your ears*.
You *can't escape it*.
Because...
...this world is burning fast.

What'ya gonna do?
Where are you gonna go?
Do you have an escape plan?
Do you have a way out?
Because...
...this world is burning fast.

"I'm going to Mars with Elon Musk!"

"The Don"
25.02.2022

Cockroaches

(Scarafaggi)

They are as dumb as fuck!
But they have it all worked out.
Just accept that you are vermin & move on.
That's what they've done.
They are happy.
They are happy to be *"Cockroaches"!*
They just wanna be *"Cockroaches"!*

They say that for every *"Cockroach"* you see...
...there are 19 you don't see!
"There!"
"I see one!"
"Do you want to kill it?"
I ask my friend.
She says...
...*"You fucking bet!"*
Grabs my thong...
...and with almighty *"whack"*...
...she squashes the *"Cockroach"*...
...FLAT!
One squashed *"Cockroach"*...
...19 to go!

It didn't stand a chance.
It never saw it coming.
It was just doing its own thing...
...being a *"Cockroach"*.
"I HATE cockroaches!"
She said, in her defence.
" I can see that!", I replied.
One less *"Cockroach"* in the world...
...a billion, trillion *"Cockroaches"* left to go!

But...
...one day, in the not too distant future.
...they will rule the Earth!

"The Don"
26.02.2022

When You Kiss Evil's Face

(Quando Baci la Faccia del Male)

Evil is *all around us.*
Evil is *stalking us.*
Evil is *hiding in the shadows.*
Beware!
Take care!
Evil is about!

Evil *surrounds us*
Evil will *haunt you.*
Evil will *take you by surprise...*
...when you are least expecting it.
Evil will *pounce when you are not looking.*
When *Evil shows its face...*
...when you come face to face with Evil...
...Do not look into its face.
...Do not look into its eyes.
...Do not let it touch you.
...Do not let it hold you.
...Do not let it embrace you.
...Do not let it kiss you.
When you kiss Evil's face...
...don't expect to walk away.
...don't expect to remain untarnished.
Because...
...when you kiss Evil's face.
...there is no turning back!

Whatever you do...
...don't kiss Evil's face.
Because...
...when you kiss Evil's face.
...there is no turning back!
...there is no turning back!
...there is no turning back!
...there is no turning BACK!!!!!

"The Don" + Miriam
27.02.2022

People Do Not Want to be Controlled
(Le Persone non Vogliono essere Controllate)

I don't want to be *controlled*.
I don't want to be *owned*.
I don't want to be *bought*.
I don't want to be a *commodity*.
I don't want to be *an object*.
I don't want to be a *possession*.
Stop!
Do not control me!
I don't want to be controlled.
People do not want to be controlled!

Do not try to *control me*.
Do not try to *own me*.
Do not try to *buy me*.
Do not treat me like a *commodity*.
Do not treat me like an *object*.
Do not treat me like a *possession*.
Stop!
Do not control me!
I don't want to be controlled.
People do not want to be controlled!

I will fight you.
You will not *win*.
You will not *control me*.
You will not *own me*.
You will not *buy me*.
I will not be your *commodity*.
I will not be your *object*.
I will not be your *possession*.
Stop!
Do not control me!
I don't want to be controlled.
People do not want to be controlled

"The Don"
28.02.2022

Screw You!

(Fottiti!)

I've got no time for your *games*.
I've got no time for your *shenanigans*.
I've got no time for your *dramas*.
I've got no time for *you!*
So...
...*screw you!*

Go & find someone else to *play with*.
Go & find someone else to *spend your time with*.
Go & find someone else to *be your new BF*.
Go & find someone else to *hang out with*.
So...
...*screw you!*

I don't need you *anymore*.
I don't need you to *talk to*.
I don't need your *body*.
I don't need you to *fuck*.
So...
...*screw you!*

"The Don"
28.02.2022

The Crying Song

(La Canzone che Piange)

It's time to cry.
The Earth is dying.
There is no one to *save it*.
There is no one who *cares*.
There no one who *dares*.
Who is going to save her?
She is all alone.
She has been forgotten...
...by everyone.
I am crying.
Because...
...this is *"The Crying Song"*.

I am crying for our *loss*.
I am crying for our *shame*.
I am crying for our *apathy*.
I am crying for our *failures*.
I am crying for our *pain*.
I am crying for our *suffering*.
I am crying or our *children*.
I am crying for our *lost humanity*.
I am crying for *myself*.
I am crying for *you*.

This is *The Crying Song*
A song in which to *pray*.
A song in which to *die*.
A song in which to *cry*.

Should we?
Shouldn't we?

"The Don" + Miriam
28.02.2022

Let the Music be your Master

(Lascia che la Musica sia il tuo Maestro)

Let the music *tell you what to do.*
Let the music *guide you where to go.*
Let the music *show you the way.*
Let the music *enter your HE♥RT.*
Let the music *permeate your soul.*
Let the music be your master.

See the music.
*Hea*r the music.
Feel the music.
Become the music.
You are the music.
Let the music be your master.

See the music in *Nature*.
Feel the music in *people*.
Feel the music in the *Universe*.
Live the music.
Let the music be your master.

04.03.2022
"The Don"

Making LO♥E

(Fare l'Amore)

To *touch*.
To *embrace*.
To *hold each other*.
To *kiss*.
To be *naked*.
Body to body.
Skin to skin.
Flesh to flesh
Breath to breath.
Lips to lips.
Tongue to tongue.
Face to face.
Connecting.
Enveloping.
Immersion.
Submerging.
Encompassing.
Submitting.
Totality.
Becoming one.
The *Oneness*.
The *completeness*.
The *Unity*.
The *coupling*.
The *desire*.
The *passion*.
The *power*.
The *energy*.
The *euphoria*.
The *spirituality*.
The *creativity*.
The *uniqueness*.
The *sensuality*.
The *experience*.

Bliss.
Ecstasy.
Happiness.
Making *music.*
Making *poetry.*
Making LO♥E.

"The Don"
07.03.2022

The Big Sleep

(Il Grande Sonno)

Wake up.
Wake up!
The Earth is burning!
The Earth being destroyed!
People are being killed.
There is war in the streets.
Humanity has gone crazy!
Humanity has gone INSANE!
Wake up.
Wake up!
From *"The Big Sleep"!*

Open your eyes.
Look around you.
Do you like what you see?
Get out of bed.
Fascists have taken over.
Psychopaths are in control.
Oligarchs are ruling the country.
Wake up.
Wake up!
From *"The Big Sleep"!*

Don't *look away.*
Don't *blink.*
Don't *close your eyes.*
Don't *turn your head.*
Don't *turn away.*
Don't *doze off.*
Don't *fall asleep.*
Don't fall into *"The Big Sleep"!*

Be *strong*.
Be *brave*.
Be *courageous*.
Be *fearless*.
Be *a warrior*.
Be *a hero*.
Be *an "Avenger"*.
Stay awake.
Stay awake.
Otherwise...
...you'll never awaken from...
... *"The Big Sleep"!*

"The Don"
07.03.2022

Youth is a Mask (but it don't last)

(La Giovinezza è una Maschera (ma non dura)

Live it *long*.
Live it *fast*.
Live it *while it lasts*
Live it in *the fast lane*.
Live it *while you can*.
You don't get a second chance.
Because...
Youth is a mask (but it don't last).

Make it *count*.
Make a *mark*.
Make a *statement*.
Make a *life*.
Don't take a wife.
Because...
Youth is a mask (but it don't last).

Have *fun*.
Have a *blast*.
Have an *adventure*.
Have a *journey*.
Have a *life*.
Because...
Youth is a mask (but it don't last).

It's better to *burn out*.
It's better *not to rust*.
It's better to *go out with a bang*.
It's better to *explode*.
It's better to *burn the candle at both ends*.
Because...
Youth is a mask (but it don't last).
Live it long & live it fast.
Because...
Youth is a mask (but it don't last).

"The Don"
13.03.2022

Bureaucracy is an Atrocity

(La Burocrazia è un'Atrocità)

Do *this*.
Don't *do that*.
Don't *go there*.
Don't *overtake*.
Don't *walk*.
Don't *run*.
Don't *stand*.
Don't *talk*.
Don't *speak*.
Don't *laugh*.
Don't *drink*.
Don't *smoke*.
Don't *be late*.
Don't *fart*.
Don't *fuck*.
Bureaucracy is an Atrocity.

Wait here.
Sign here.
Sit here.
Stand here.
Stand behind the yellow line.
Get in line.
Be *quiet*.
Be *still*.
Be *serious*.
Be *professional*.
Be *on time*.
Speak when you are spoken to.
Follow the *rules*.
Follow the *laws*.
Follow *instructions*
Do what you are told.
Bureaucracy is an Atrocity.

Bureaucracy run riot!

"The Don"
13.03.2022

Birthplace (Origins)

(Luogo di Nascita (Origini))

He was born in a small village.
High on the side of a mountain.
Called *"San Fele"*.
In the southern region of *"Basilicata"*, Italy.
Its capital is called *"Potenza"*.
It means *"Strength"* in English.
And maybe there is some truth in this.
The people from this region are a proud & resilient bunch.
Authentic.
They've experienced the pitfalls, hardships & tribulations that life throws at you.
You can see it etched on their faces.
But they are survivors.
They are as tough as steel & then some.
But they are also humble folk.
No time for pretentiousness here.
Whatever they have, which is not much...
...they'll gladly share it with *"paesane"*.
If you happen to walk by.

They worked the land.
That unforgiving earth.
Removing stones with their bare hands.
And carrying them away on their backs.
They still ploughed the land with a cow drawn plough in 1964.
Life was tough.
As touch as it comes.
Some might even call it *"brutal"*.
But they had no other way to live...
...to survive.
This was their life.
This had been their life.

Until one day his whole world was about to change...
...forever.
With his mother & older brother, they immigrated to Sydney, Australia.
"The land of milk & honey".
"The promised land."
There he was reunited with his father that he had never seen before.
Life was tough for him.

But this was not new.
He had always had a tough life.
He knew what he had to do...
...to survive & prosper in this unforsaken backwater.

Then one day, in 1972.
A film was released called *"The Godfather"*.
A film considered by many to be one of the best films ever made.
High praise indeed.
The main character *"The Godfather"*, was called *"The Don"*...
...*"I'll Padrino"*.
...*"The Godfather"*
His name was *"Don Vito Corleone"!*

And so, his identity was chosen for him.
His friends soon started to call him *"Don"*.
He liked it.
It stuck.
"The Don" was born!

San Fele, Basilicata, Italy

"The Don"
14.03 2022

Don't Let the Grass Grow Under Your Feet
(Non Fare L'erba Cresca Sotto i tuoi Piedi)

Don't stand still.
Move.
Take risks.
Challenge yourself.
Walk on the wild side.
Dance in the sunshine.
Sing in the rain.
Fly on the wind.
Jump into puddles.
Run with the tigers.
Eat with lions.
Swim with the sharks.
Be wild.
Be CRAZY!
Be mad.
Let your hair grow.
Let it all hang out.
Go naked.
Dive into the deep end.
Jump the fence.
Look around corners.
Shout from the rooftops.
Climb mountains.
Laugh with the monkeys.
Stretch your neck like the giraffes.
Break down the wall.
Enter the *"Dragons Lair"*.
Go into the *"Heart of Darkness"*.
Breathe in the *"Light"*.
Smoke the *"Sacred Bush"*.
Sleep with the *"Sirens"*.
Fight the *"Minotaur"*.
FUCK like an animal.
Wake up to a new morning.
"Seize the day!"
But whatever you do....
...*don't let the grass grow under your feet.*

Unless of course it's *"weed"*!

"The Don"
19.03.2022

Plutonic LO♥E

(Amore Platonico)

Is there such a thing?
Does it exist?
And if it does...
...what does it look like?
This thing called...?
..."Plutonic LO♥E"?

LO♥E without *passion*.
LO♥E without *fire*.
LO♥E without *intimacy*.
LO♥E without *LO♥E*.
Is this...
..."Plutonic LO♥E"?

I don't know if I like it!

"The Don"
19.03.2022

Commitment

(Impegno)

Is it an *obligation*?
Is it *misplaced loyalty*?
Is it a *noose around your neck*?
Is it a *chain that holds you down*?
Is it an *albatross you carry with you*?
Is it a *burden you have to bear*?
Is it a *part you no longer want to play*?
Is it a *film you no longer want to be in*?
Is it as if *seeing with new eyes*?
Is it as if *seeing clearly for the very first time*?
Is it a *dream that's turned into a nightmare*?
Is it *a full glass that is now empty*?
Is it a *house that is no longer a home*?
Is it a *home that now has become a prison*?
Is it a *passion that now is an abyss*?
Is it a *desire that has now become a repulsion*?
Is it a *pleasure that now has become a pain*?
Is it a *happiness that has become a sadness*?
Is it a LO♥E that is no longer "forever after"?
Is it a LO♥ER that now has become a DEVIL?
Is it a *pleasurable arrangement that has now become a commitment*?

Commitment...
...who needs it?
No one!

"The Don"
21.03.2022

RESPECT

(RISPETTO)

Reciprocity.

Equality.

Symbiosis.

Partnership.

Empathy

Care.

Togetherness.

RESPECT *others.*
RESPECT *yourself.*
RESPECT *out!*
RESPECT...
...that's what it's all about!

"The Don"
21.03.2022

Sympathy for the Devil

(Simpatia per il Diavolo)

Have some *respect*.
Have some *decency*.
Have some *fear*.
Have some sympathy for the Devil.

Watch out.
Take care.
Run & hide.
Have some sympathy for the Devil.

It's *here*.
It's in *control*.
It's *powerful*.
So...
...have some sympathy for the Devil.

There's *nothing you can do*.
There's *nowhere to run*.
There's *nowhere to hide*.
So...
...have some sympathy for the Devil.

Accept your *fate*.
Accept your *destiny*.
Accept your *life*.
Accept your *DEATH*.
So...
...have some sympathy for the Devil.

"The Don"
21.03.2022

Sometimes This World Makes Me Crazy

(A Volte Questo Mondo mi fa Impazzire)

Too much *confusion*.
Too much *traffic*.
Too much *noise*.
Too much *pollution*.
Too much *greed*.
Too much *exploitation*.
Too much *violence*.
Too much *abuse*.
Too much *hatred*
Too many *rules*.
Too many *choices*.
Too many *people*.
Too many *arguments*.
Too many *wars*.
Too many *crazies*.
Too little *time*.
Too few *choices*.
Too little *respect*.
Too little *kindness*.
Too little *compassion*.
Too little *humanity*.

"The Don"
22.03.2022

(Capriccio)

Do you *belong here?*
Do you *stand out from the crowd?*
Do you *do your own thing?*
Do you *feel that you don't belong?*
Do you *feel like you don't fit in?*
Do you feel *rejected?*
Do you feel *abandoned?*
Do you feel *alone?*
Do you feel like you're an *"Outsider"?*
Do you hate *society?*
Do you hate *politicians?*
Do you hate *governments?*
Do you hate *"Capitalism"?*
Do you hate *consumerism?*
Do you hate *"Communism"?*
Do you hate *"Fascism"?*

Don't worry...
...you're not alone.

You are an "Alien".

You are a "Freak"!

"The Don"
23.03.2022

Living in a World of Make-Believe
(Vivere una Terra di Finzione)

We're living in a world of *make-believe*.
We're living in a world of *fantasy*.
We're living in a world of *myths*.
We're living in a world of *fakeness*.
We're living in a world of *stupidity*.
We're living in a world of *lunacy*.
We're living in a world of *idiots*.
We're living in a world of *madness*.
We're living in a world of *confusion*.
We're living in a world of *sadness*.
We're living in a world of *loneliness*.
We're living in a world of *sorrow*.
We're living in a world of *individuality*.
We're living in a world of *consumerism*.
We're living in a world of *propaganda*.
We're living in a world of *manipulation*.
We're living in a world of *lies*.
We're living in a world of *control*.
We're living in a world of *obedience*.
We're living in a world of *punishment*.
We're living in a world of *HORROR!*

The Don"
23.03.2022

Too Emotional, Too Romantic

(Troppo Emotivo, Troppo Romantico)

That's what I am.
That's what I've been told.
Too emotional, too romantic.

Is that such a bad thing?
Is that such an awful thing.
To be...
...too emotional, too romantic.

I don't think so.
I think it's a beautiful.
To be...
...too emotional, too romantic.

Try it.
You might like it.
To be...
...too emotional, too romantic.

Be emotional.
Be romantic.
There's nothing wrong with being...
...too emotional, too romantic.

Embrace being...
...too emotional, too romantic.

The Don"
23.03.2022

Make LOVE Not War!
(Fate l'Amore non Fate la Guerra!)

Make
LOVE
Not War!

"Make love, not war" is an anti-war slogan commonly associated with the American counterculture of the 1960s. It was used primarily by those who were opposed to the Vietnam War, but has been invoked in other anti-war contexts since, around the world. The "Make love" part of the slogan often referred to the practice of free love that was growing among the American youth who denounced marriage as a tool for those who supported war and favoured the traditional capitalist culture."
https://en.wikipedia.org/wiki/Make_love,_not_war

"The Don"
25.03.2022

"Turn On, Tune In, Drop Out"
("Accendi, Sintonizzati, Esci")

"Turn on, tune in, drop out"

Quote from Dr Timothy Leary, 1967

(Timothy Francis Leary (22 October 1920 – 31 May 1996) was an American writer, psychologist, campaigner for psychedelic drug research and use, 1960s counterculture icon and computer software designer. He is most famous as a proponent of the therapeutic and spiritual benefits of LSD. During the 1960s, he coined and popularized the catch phrase "Turn on, tune in, drop out.")
https://en.wikiquote.org/wiki/Timothy_Leary

"The Don"
25.03.2022

Today's Lesson is...

(La Lezione di Oggi è...)

To...
...listen.
...hear.
...see.
...think.
...feel.
...imagine.
...act.

That's today's lesson.

This is your homework...
To...
...listen.
...hear.
...see.
...think.
...feel.
...imagine.
...act.

Make sure you all do it.
I will be making it out of 10.
And your mark will go towards determining your assessment mark.

On whether you have passed as a *"Human Being"*.

"Good luck!"
"You will need it."

"The Don"
25.03.2022

Books written by "The Don"

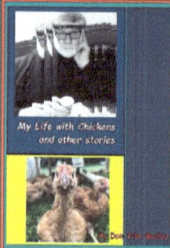

"My Life with Chickens & other stories: I Pity the Poor Immigrant"
Published:
10th September, 2019
Autobiography Book 1:
0 – 12 years old

"Poems for Misfits, Miscreants, Misanthropes, Mavericks, Losers & Malcontents!"
Published:
10th June, 2020
Book of Poems 1

"Poems for Troubled Minds & Trouble Hearts"
Published:
10th August, 2020

Book of Poems 2

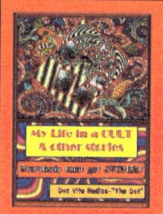

"My Life in a CULT & other stories: Everybody Must Get STONED!"
Published:
10th September, 2020
Autobiography Book 2:
15 – 30 years old

"Poems for Restless Minds & Restless Hearts"
Published:
10th October, 2020
Book of Poems 3

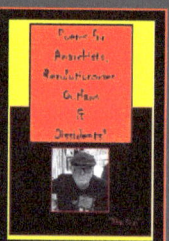

"Poems for Anarchists, Revolutionaries, Outlaws & Dissidents!"
Published:
10th November, 2020

Book of Poems 4

"Poems for Non-Thinkers & Eccentrics"
Published:
10th December, 2020
Book of Poems 5

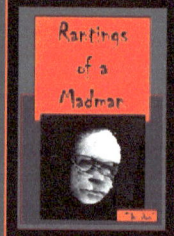

"The Rantings of a Madman"
Published:
10th January, 2021

Book of Poems 6

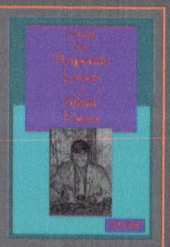

"Poems for Desperate Lovers & Silent Voices"
Published:
10th February, 2021
Book of Poems 7

"Poems for Tormented Minds & Tortured Souls"
Published:
10th March, 2021
Book of Poems 8

All available ONLY online

Books written by "The Don"

"Poems for ALIENS, Outsiders, Outcasts & other STRANGE BEINGS!"
Published: 10th April, 2021
Book of Poems 9

"Poems for Beings From Another Planet"
Published: 10th May, 2021
Book of Poems 10

"Poems for Mindless Beings & Lost Souls"
Published: 10th June, 2021
Book of Poems 11

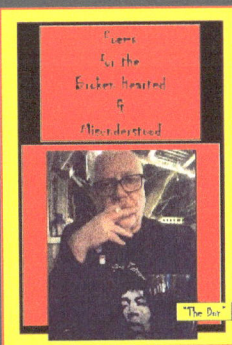

"Poems for the Broken Hearted & Misunderstood
Published: 10th July, 2021
Book of Poems 12

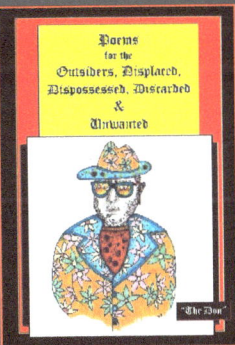

"Poems for Poems for the Bewildered, Dazed & Confused"
10th August, 2021
Book of Poems 13

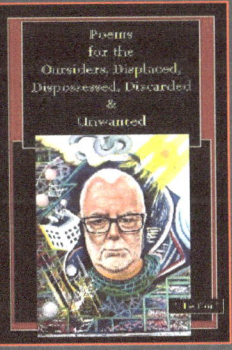

"Poems for the Outsiders, Displaced, Dispossessed, Discarded & Unwanted"
Published: 10th Sept, 2021
Book of Poems 14

All available ONLY online

"Poems for Secret Agents, Phantom Agents, Agents of Change, Agent Provocateurs & Agents of Chaos"
Published: 10th Oct, 2021
Book of Poems 15

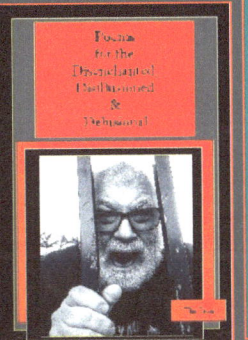

"Poems for Disenchanted, Disillusioned & Delusional"
Published: 10th November, 2021
Book of Poems 16

Books written by "The Don"

"Poems for the Stoners, drugos, ACID takers & Psychedelic LO♥ERS (Everybody Must Get Stoned)"
Published: 10th December, 2021
Book of Poems 17

"Poems for Anarchists, Rebels & Revolutionaries
Published: 10th January, 2022
Book of Poems 18

"Poems for Rebels, Radicals & Revolutionaries (Viva la Révolution!)"
Published: 10th February, 2022
Book of Poems 19

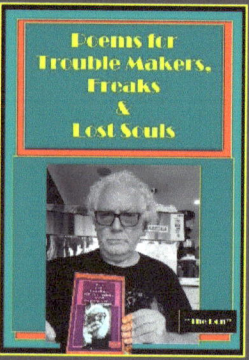

"Poems for Trouble Makers, Freaks & Lost Souls"
Published: 10th March 2022
Book of Poems 20

"Poems for Zombies & the Walking Dead"
Published: 10th April 2022
Book of Poems 21

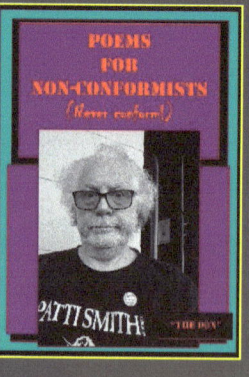

"Poems for Non-Conformists (Never conform!)"
Published: 10th May 2022
Book of Poems 22

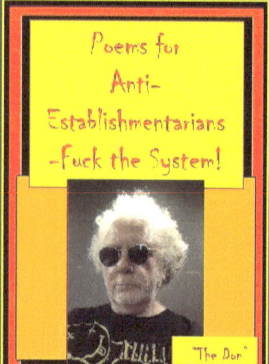

"Poems for Anti-Establishmentarians-Fuck the System!"

Published: 10th June 2022

Book of Poems 23

Vito Radice ("The Don")
(Poet/Author/Polemicist/Non-Thinker/Non-Intellectual)
Email: vitoradice@gmail.com
Instagram: don_vito_radice
Facebook: Vito Radice
Mobile: +61490012461
(Australia)

www.ingramcontent.com/pod-product-compliance
Lightning Source LLC
Chambersburg PA
CBHW042048290426
44109CB00006B/150